Freedom from Addiction

Turning from Your
Addictive Behavior

Edward T. Welch

New
Growth
Press
www.newgrowthpress.com

All Scripture quotations, unless otherwise indicated, are taken from the *Holy Bible,* New International Version®, NIV®. Copyright © 1973, 1978, 1984 by International Bible Society. Used by permission of Zondervan. All rights reserved.

New Growth Press, Greensboro, NC 27404
Copyright © 2008 by Christian Counseling & Educational Foundation. All rights reserved. Published 2008

Cover Design: The DesignWorks Group, Nate Salciccioli and Jeff Miller, www.thedesignworksgroup.com

Typesetting: Robin Black, www.blackbirdcreative.biz

ISBN: 978-1-939946-59-1 (Print)
ISBN: 978-1-934885-44-4 (eBook)

Library of Congress Cataloging-in-Publication Data

Welch, Edward T., 1953-
  Freedom from addiction : turning from your addictive behavior / Edward T. Welch.
      p. cm.
  Includes bibliographical references and index.
  ISBN 978-1-934885-44-4
  1. Compulsive behavior—Religious aspects—Christianity.
  2. Addicts—Religious life. I. Title.
  BV4598.7.W45 2008
  248.8'629—dc22

                                        2008011936

Printed in Canada
21 20 19 18 17 16 15 14   1 2 3 4 5

I f you are struggling with an addiction to a substance or to an activity, you already know a lot. Experience is a good teacher. You might not be an expert on how to get *out* of addiction, but you certainly know what it's like to have one, so you might resist anyone who wants to instruct you. But you *are* reading this, which means you are trying to stay open and teachable. Please keep trying.

The brief article that follows will stretch your understanding of your addiction. It will sound radical—anything that brings Jesus into your world will be subversive and contrary to your expectations. But it will make sense. God is the source of all wisdom, and when we understand his wisdom it sounds true, right, and good. So suspend your judgment for a moment. You might be an expert *in* your addiction, but consider the possibility that the God who made you knows best how to help you *out* of your addiction. Don't just read the following comments. Wrestle with them; argue with them; and don't stop wrestling and arguing until you find new and fresh hope in Jesus.

Why You Do Your Addiction

You do your addiction because you like it, or more accurately because you love it. We do the things we love, and we avoid doing the things we hate. Your addiction first attracted your attention, next you became infatuated, and then love grew. What you didn't anticipate is that love, whenever it is self-centered, matures into worship, and you are a slave to what you worship. This explains why you both desire your addiction and find that it's a weight around your neck. Having an addiction means you are worshiping something and are controlled by it. It owns you. You think about it, plot how you will get more of it, dream about it when you don't have it, and are willing to sacrifice almost anything to get it. This is how the Bible explains it: "For a man is a slave to whatever has mastered him" (2 Peter 2:19).

Your Addiction Is About You and God

If addiction is truly a form of worship, then it shouldn't surprise you that it has something to do with God. This doesn't mean you are thinking about God all the time. Addiction never seems personal. For example, if you are married you don't think about your spouse in the midst of your addiction, but addiction is about your spouse. The lying, deceit, financial toll, and betrayal are all about your spouse. Even more so, your addiction is about you and God. The reality is that all of life is tied to God. Everything you do, if you really think about it, is about God.

When you try to avoid God and worship something other than him, you become a slave to what you are worshiping. Worship sex—become its slave. Worship cocaine—be owned by it. That's the way

God's universe is constructed. It's all about our allegiances. When your allegiance is to something other than God, you will simultaneously feel both in control and out of control. You will love your addiction and hate it. You will feel both alive and dead.

Welcome to the reality of sin. All false worship is sin; and sin, when you keep practicing it, will oppress you. Sin is the real diagnosis for addiction. Genetics, parents, peers, and many other factors can contribute, but the root is sin. This is not an immediate self-esteem enhancer, to be sure, but it is much more hopeful than you might think. Sin is humanity's root problem, and at the deepest places in your soul you are no different from anyone else. Sin is the root of all addiction.

Your Biggest Problem Is Not Your Addiction

No doubt you know that you sin once in a while, but you might be reluctant to call your addiction sin. Sin, we think, is conscious rebellion against God, and what you are doing doesn't feel that way. Yet take this critical first step: Acknowledge that addiction is against God. Sin is when you worship anything other than the true God. Sin is voluntary. We choose it. And it is also slavery. It dominates us. We need to turn from it *and* be delivered from it. But is your addictive behavior your biggest sin? No, but it does point to your biggest problem: your lack of relationship with the God who made you. Consider what your addiction says about your relationship to God.

- You believe you can manage your world apart from God.
- You believe there are places where you can hide from God. You think God is like a person, only stronger, with more acute senses. Notice this: If you were being

shadowed by someone extremely important to you—a spouse, a parent, a boss, a
child—you probably wouldn't be doing
your addiction in the way you are now.
Addictions thrive in the dark, where you
think God can't see you. Maybe you can
relate to the psalmist who said, "Surely
the darkness will hide me." And then he
noticed that he couldn't hide from God,
because "even the darkness will not be dark
to you; the night will shine like the day"
(Psalm 139:11–12).

• You love your addiction more than you
love God. You think there are things more
beautiful and satisfying than him.

The bottom line is that you want to be God.
You have constructed a world that revolves around
you and your desires, not around God. Your biggest

sin is your desire to be your own god—this is what fuels your addiction. You have broken the first commandment: "You shall have no other gods before me" (Exodus 20:3).

Be willing to feel the weight of your rebellion against God, but don't stop there. One of the many beautiful features of God revealed in the Bible is that he is the forgiving God. Here is one of his many promises to forgive those who ask: "If we claim to be without sin, we deceive ourselves and the truth is not in us. If we confess our sins, he is faithful and just and will forgive us our sins and purify us from all unrighteousness. If we claim we have not sinned, we make him out to be a liar and his word has no place in our lives" (1 John 1:8–10).

Do you see how hopeful this is? If your addiction is an unconquerable compulsion, then you are stuck; but if your biggest problem is that you are a sinner, there is hope. Jesus came into our world, died a terrible death, and rose again to save sinners. You can have a whole new life simply by admitting that you are a sinner and you need Jesus to save you. This is called true faith or trust. You can learn to live by faith as you struggle with your addiction.

Practical Strategies for Change

Putting your faith in Jesus will gradually transform your whole life. What are some practical ways that you can live out your faith in the midst of your struggle with addiction? Here are a few things you should start doing right now.

Speak Honestly

Lies are the natural language of addiction. You have told a boatload. You have told lies to others. You have also told lies to yourself—blatant whoppers—and you have believed them. Do these sound familiar?

"I can stop any time I want."

"I'm not like *those* people (other addicts). I would never _____ (use needles, drink alone, use my children's food money, drink on the job, watch sadistic pornography)."

Your lies are fueled by your pride, and they persist because of your shame. Now they are instinctive. In the beginning you might have noticed when you were lying, but after a while your conscience quieted down. Now lies are your natural speech—and you don't even notice. Lies have become so natural that sometimes you lie even when the truth would work better.

Lies are the language of a particular kingdom. "When he [Satan] lies, he speaks his native language, for he is a liar and the father of lies" (John 8:44). When you speak, you reveal your allegiances. When you speak the truth, you are taking a first step toward the kingdom of God. When you lie, you are digging in your heels and preferring the comfort of darkness and the sense of independence that are part of Satan's kingdom. Here is where you must act. You have to stop being a robot, controlled by your addiction, and make a decision. (You already made a significant decision when you chose to read this.) Pray for the power to speak the truth, and then start to tell the truth. Tell the truth to one person. The apostle Paul wrote in Ephesians that step one for someone leaving an addictive life is to "put off falsehood and speak truthfully to his neighbor, for we are all members of one body" (Ephesians 4:25).

Go Public

When you begin to understand the wisdom of God, you will find that humility is one of its most important aspects. Humility means acknowledging your need for help. Ask God for help, and then, since God uses people to extend his help to us, ask other people for help. Do this before you come up with twenty reasons why you shouldn't. Your reasons might sound selfless (for example, you don't want to embarrass or shame family members). But ignore your excuses. Run from them.

Get a Plan

Do you want to change? Evaluate your resolve by developing a plan and implementing it. Be radical, ruthless, and forceful (Matthew 5:29–30; 11:12). If you are hoping that your addiction will go away without a fight, then you don't really want to get rid of it. When you look for a job you don't say, "God, beam me to the right job today while I watch TV." Instead, you make a plan. In the same way, you need a strategy for how you will fight your addiction. Ask for help, and once again, be suspicious of any of your excuses.

Make Jesus Central

You probably know that most treatments for addiction include "god as you understand him." You have many options for this "god," but be careful. If you invent your own god, you will have the same problem you always had: you trying to be god. You need something way more powerful than your conception of God, which is only a mix of your desires and fears. You need to know THE God. There is only one God who could never be invented by our desires. The true God delights in being known. He is the only God who entered human history and humbled himself to become a part of his creation. THE God has revealed himself in Jesus Christ. Jesus is "the radiance of God's glory and the exact representation of his being" (Hebrews 1:3). If your eyes aren't on him, you will be lured from one form of false worship and slavery to another.

God has determined that *real* change must go through Jesus. Anything else would dishonor him. Try to change apart from Jesus and you might remove a few hassles from your own kingdom, but you will eventually be enslaved to something else. The next addiction might be safer, but it will still dominate you. Real change happens when you confess your sin, ask Jesus for forgiveness, and then live with Jesus' death, resurrection, and growing kingdom at the center of your everyday life.

To make Jesus central you will need help. You will need to read the Bible. God speaks in various ways, but his clearest and most common communication to us is through the Bible. The story of Jesus' life, death, and resurrection in the Book of Mark is a good place to start. Also find others who follow Jesus. You probably already know someone who does. If not, ask around. Look for people who believe that Jesus is THE God who came to earth, died for our sins, and rose from the dead.

Find a Church

What does a church have to do with addictions? A good church is like AA, but better because it points you to Jesus. Remember, God's wise plan is to use people to help us. He uses a community. You were not created to be isolated, and you weren't created to change apart from a community. If you have no leads on a church, check your phone book and look for churches that say something about Jesus Christ in their advertising.

Live with Hope

Don't believe Satan's lie that you can't change. After you read the Book of Mark, read through Acts and you will see that people do change. When Jesus Christ ascended to his throne in heaven he sent his

Spirit. The Spirit is the Spirit of power, and he makes us look more and more like Jesus.

When you are filled with the Spirit, your desires will gradually change, and you will begin to live a beautiful and fruitful life of love toward God and others. When you daily repent of trying to be your own god, daily ask God to fill you with his Spirit, and daily take the steps of faith outlined above, then you will see that God is present and active in your life.

So can you change? Absolutely. You should tremble at the thought of God working in you (Philippians 2:12–13). The process, however, will seem like two steps forward and one step back. It is gradual. If it was any other way, you wouldn't have to depend on Jesus all the time—which is exactly what he wants you to do. If change is particularly stubborn, ask yourself this question: Do I really want to change? You will find all kinds of reasons why you aren't changing, but this question might point you to the real culprit.

Don't be surprised when you fall back into temptation, but remember that God's compassions are new every morning (Lamentations 3:21–23). Every morning you can repent of your sins, ask for the Spirit of God, and begin again to live by faith. Every Christian is called to do these things every day. Why don't you join them?

Simple, Quick, Biblical

Advice on Complicated Counseling Issues
for Pastors, Counselors, and Individuals

MINIBOOK
CATEGORIES

- Personal Change
- Marriage & Parenting
- Medical & Psychiatric Issues
- Women's Issues
- Singles
- Military

USE YOURSELF | GIVE TO A FRIEND | DISPLAY IN YOUR CHURCH OR MINISTRY

New Growth Press

Go to **www.newgrowthpress.com** or call **336.378.7775** to
purchase individual minibooks or the entire collection.
Durable acrylic display stands are also available to house
the minibook collection.